The Secrets of the Ume

The Secrets of the Ume

Japanese Pickled Plum

Dr. Moriyasu Ushio, M.D.

Translation by
Jacques de Langre, Ph. D.

Happiness Press
Magalia, California

The original text is by Dr. Moriyasu Ushio M.D. The cartoons are by the artist: Kamakiri Uno. The original book, *The Secret of the Umeboshi* ,was published by Shinpyosha Publishing, Japan. The initial translation into French was completed in 1975 by Clim Yoshimi & Guy de Frouville. The authorized English translation is by Jacques de Langre, Ph.D.

Printed in Hong Kong   ISBN# 0-916508-40-4

Happiness Press
P.O. Box DD
Magalia CA 95954
(916) 873-0294

CONTENTS

Why the Ume Works

The Umeboshi salted plum stimulates the secretion of the parotid hormone, a known rejuvenating substance. This hormone, secreted in small amounts by the salivary glands (the submaxillae and the parotids), readily mixes in the blood stream, promotes tissue function as well as activates the metabolism. Eating one or two Umes every day is an excellent way of preventing aging of the cells.

An oldster who has reached 101 years of age goes to help his grandson, running all the way for two kilometers of mountainous trails on his way to this grandson's house. His daily consumption of two Umes appears to be a good part of the secret of his stamina and longevity.

The Umeboshi possesses an incontestable capability to stimulate salivation. Most Japanese people will automatically salivate at the mere sight or mention of an Umeboshi.

ACTIVE INGREDIENTS

The Ume is made from a special strain of plum that is never consumed in its unripe green state because, at that stage, the inside of the pit contains a certain amount of amygdalin,[1] which is a

1. Amygdalin: A white, bitter tasting, water-soluble glycosidic powder, obtained from various plants: medicinally used chiefly as an expectorant.

glycoside of hydrocyanic acid.[2]

When ripe, however, the ume fruit no longer contains any of this amygdalin and the pickling of this green fruit renders it also totally free of this detrimental substance.

Mishizane or Tenjin? One of the polytheist lords respected at a shrine demonstrates that the pit of the ume yields a nut that demands our respect. It contains: Laetril, B17. The excess of cyanic acid is totally eliminated from the nut inside the pit of the dried ume.

NUTRIENTS

Amongst all fruits, the Ume is the richest in nutrients. It contains many proteins, calcium, phosphorus, iron, and some organic acids such as citric, malic, succinic and tartaric acids. For more about the advantages of these acids, see chapter 2.

The ume alkalinizes the blood. According to the theory of acid and alkaline, chronic disease is caused by the acidification of the blood and of the cellular tissues. This condition can be accurately measured by the pH of the patient's body fluids. The scale measuring pH, or hydrogen ion concentration runs from 0 to 14. However, 7 is the neutral point and the pH of distilled water. The pH of a healthy person's blood is 7.35, whereas in a sick person the blood measures 7.30. Although this is only a .05 increase in acidity, this condition invites trouble, since this slight acidity excess allows tissues and organs to easily become inflamed.

The acidic blood condition, called acidosis leads to various infectious diseases, liver illness and aging problems such as

2. Hydrocyanic acid or Hydrogen cyanide is a poisonous gas that has a bitter, almond-like odor.

neuralgia, rheumatism, cerebral hemorrhages, gastric ulcers and hypertension. Acidosis is very prevalent today and unless this excess of acidity is corrected by a proper diet all remedies are futile.

Modern dietetic science recognizes five elements that need to be present in order to maintain good health:

1 - glycogen,
2 - protein,
3 - fats,
4 - vitamins and
5 - minerals.

These nutrients do not readily change into energy, they must first go through several transmutations. It is here that the citric acid plays its important role.

CITRIC ACID AND ITS ROLE

Citric acid is a compound that helps in the oxidation of fats, proteins and carbohydrates, changing them to carbon dioxide and water (see footnote, page 6).

Professor Krebs of Sheffield University studied the value of the Japanese umeboshi and has clarified many facets of its mechanism of nutrition. In the citric acid cycle of Krebs, glycogen breaks down due to the presence of citric acid and the vitality increases because energy is then abundantly produced.

This demonstrates that the umeboshi is more than a simple nutrient, because it acts as a catalyst.

Five Beneficial Effects

I — ILLNESSES OF OLD AGE
ARE EFFECTIVELY PREVENTED

In order to truly enjoy a long life, one should not have to suffer from any of the illnesses of aging. Because the ume triggers the secretion of parotin hormone, it effectively prevents age-related illnesses.

Old age can use the hormone parotin, which is in salivary glands. How soon will the ume lollipop shown here become a reality for retired people?

II — BLOOD CLEANSING

Most modern people consume refined staples such as polished cereal grain products, white bread, pasta, white sugar, chemical spices and adulterants, etc., as well as animal products. These foods cause the blood to become laden with toxins, in time causing a stagnation of the circulatory system that creates an acidic condition. One umeboshi taken every day cleanses the blood, restores optimum blood flow while naturally purging the organism of excess acidity.

III — INCREASE IN VITALITY

Acceleration of the metabolism together with blood cleansing restores vitality. When the citric acid cycle performs smoothly and stimulates the metabolism properly, the excess acid generated by wrong foods cannot remain in the organism. Additionally, vitamins and enzymes are better utilized. These are the reasons why the umeboshi increases vitality and strength thus building resistance to disease and fatigue.

IV — A POWERFUL INTERNAL DISINFECTANT

In former times in Japan, epidemics of dysentery and typhoid were effectively fought by administering umeboshi plums. Umeboshis have a sterilization power two hundred times greater than a 40% solution of formaldehyde.[1] Ume, however are free of the toxicity of formaldehyde. There is an additional advantage because the umeboshi is also an anti-putrefactive agent. Recently it has been discovered that the ume extract, or a concentration of ume plums, possess an even greater cleansing or sanitizing power than formaldehyde.

V — BAN FATIGUE

The statement, "I am tired", physiologically means only that certain detrimental acid substances are present in the body. If an umeboshi

---

1. Formaldehyde or Methanal possesses an extreme reactivity with proteins. This feature is the basis for its use as an embalming agent, a soil sterilant and a powerful disinfectant. It is, however, a dangerous irritant to the mucous membranes.

is taken when tired; fatigue is immediately relieved; partly by the stimulating action of the salt, but also by the natural and beneficial acids of the ume: citric,[2] pyruvic,[3] and lactic[4] acids that destroy the harmful ones.

The fatigue caused by moist and oppressive heat is relieved by a macrobiotic diet and an ume helps too.

2. Citric acid is a compound that helps in the oxidation of fats, proteins and carbohydrates, changing them to carbon dioxide and water.

3. Pyruvic acid: Dr. Krebs discovered that food converts into pyruvic acid by glycolysis, the acid then enters the citric acid cycle, each transformation in turn releasing more energy. However, if the cycle flow is broken, excess pyruvic acid is produced which then automatically converts into a surplus of lactic acid that pollutes the cells, causing fatigue and premature aging. A toxic accumulation of lactic acid (0.25 to 0.4%) causes muscle cramps, shoulder and neck aches. When the citric acid cycle works correctly, blood remains alkaline and the muscles remain flexible and cramp-free. The craving for lemons by active workers and athletes is a sign of citric acid requirement but a better way is the taking of an ume plum as it supplies a better form of citric, plus the lactic and pyruvic acids. The role of these acids in the fermentative processes is recognized in natural medicine. Dr. Krebs was awarded the 1953 Nobel prize in biochemistry.

4. Lactic acid (the positively charged- cathion type) plays an important and beneficial role in the transformation of carbohydrates, but there is another form, negatively charged (anion) that occurs in blood under stress.

Ume Is Ready to Help

In the following applications, the useful role of the Ume is studied.

1 — ARTERIOSCLEROSIS

Old age illnesses are arteriosclerosis, hypertension, kidney problems, liver diseases, diabetes and rheumatism which are all caused by increased cholesterol in the blood. Excess cholesterol hardens the arteries and speeds up aging.

With the help of the Ume, we can reduce the high cholesterol in foods.

It is always advisable to reduce the intake of foods high in cholesterol, such as meat, fish, and dairy products and to take one or two umeboshi plums each day to eliminate the excess of cholesterol. Even at a young age, toxin-producing foods should be replaced by cereal grains, vegetables, seaweeds and legumes such as beans and umeboshi plums. All these staple foods may be prepared with small amounts of unsaturated vegetable oil that contains the right amount of beneficial linoleic acid.[1]

2 — HYPERTENSION

Today, even elementary school children suffer from hypertension. This is caused by the drastic changes in modern diet and food choice. It is a fallacy to think that hypertension at any age can be prevented by avoiding salt. Salt is a regulator of many bodily functions yet its consumption should always be moderate but consist only of natural light gray unrefined sea salt.

The corrective diet should consist of whole brown rice and other grains, seasoned with sesame salt or unsalted but with the accompanying vegetables seasoned with natural soy sauce. The specific daily treatment for hypertension consists of one or two halves of umeboshi soaked for a few minutes in lukewarm water or bancha tea and sipped.

3 — CHRONIC LACK OF APPETITE

A continuous lack of appetite can only be caused by a malfunction of certain organs. Drastic weight loss caused by the oppressive heat of summer indicates that the liver, stomach and colon are not functioning well. However, the temporary lack of appetite can also be the result of overeating or chronic worrying.

Poor appetite is also common after an illness or while convalescing. In such a case the patient must try to restore his zest for food, for a good appetite will ensure the recovery of strength. An umeboshi daily is very helpful in such a case. Even for persons in good health the umeboshi has a role as appetizer.

---

1. One of the fatty acids that cannot be synthesized by humans and should be supplemented in the diet.

4 — CUTS IN THE MOUTH, COMMISSURAL STOMATITIS

An inflammation of the mouth caused by an excess of yin food intake, such as sweets, sugar, soft drinks, ice cream and tropical fruits. Stomatitis is quite painful and damaging to the whole system.

Stomach troubles or ulcerated stomach?
Instead of surgery, an ume every morning . . .

Although modern medicine and dieticians prescribe a diet high in vitamin B_{12}, such as whole wheat, sauerkraut, pickles, celery, or spinach, this disease is cured faster by eating daily a roasted umeboshi.

5 — CONSTIPATION

Good elimination is evidence of good health. The umeboshi is an effective laxative because its pectic acid draws to the colon the optimum quantity of fluids in order to insure proper formation of the feces. Pectic acid is usually obtained from apples; the umeboshi, however, contains the right amount of pectin in its skin, in spite of three days and night of salt-curing.

Relieve constipation with the habit of an ume in
the morning.

Pectic acid accelerates the peristaltic action of the intestine while disinfecting it of pathological organisms. It also serves to hasten the breakdown of proteins. The smooth normalized functioning of the digestive tract triggered by the umeboshi will put an end to constipation. As a fast cure for constipation, an umeboshi taken in warm water or bancha tea, on arising, will readily achieve the proper results.

6 — BAD BREATH OR HALITOSIS

Various unpleasant odors that originate from the mouth are either caused by inflamed buccal membranes, alveolar pyorrhea, caries, defective teeth, or unbalanced microbial flora in the saliva. These unpleasant smells may also come from food particles remaining in the mouth, but quite often bad breath originates from strong fermentation that arise from the stomach or even from the intestines. In the latter cases, chronic bad breath is a sign of a malfunction of the digestive tract, and the offensive breath will not disappear with superficial mouthwash or perfumed sweet shots of oral sprays. The umeboshi attacks the source of the trouble and is thus the most effective medium for eradicating bad breath at its source.

7 — INFANTILE DYSENTERY, TYPHOID, OR ACUTE DYSENTERY

A medical report shows that the S-shaped cholera bacteria, vibrio, dies after being immersed five minutes in umeboshi extract, the Ebert bacillus is destroyed by the same solution in twenty to thirty minutes, and the dysentery bacillus is killed in an hour. These diseases have almost disappeared due to the widespread use of modern antibiotics.

However, the indiscriminate use of antibiotics has created a dysenter bacillus that resists these antibiotics, and the improved strains has become totally resistant. For that reason, and also because the umeboshi carries no side-effects, nor depletes the body's own defenses; when faced with exposure to dysentery or even typhoid, it is safer to rely on a daily intake of the beneficial umeboshi to prevent or cure these.

The traditional street vendor cries: "Ume, Ume!" The ume is part of japanese tradition and life, but when an infectious epidemic strikes, the street vendor of Ume becomes a very popular sight and is a successful merchant.

8 — HANGOVER

Troubles caused by imbibing wine or liquor to excess are very real and quite painful. Symptoms such as nausea, dizziness or vertigo, as well as a vague feeling of inertial and listlessness are experienced. Here also quick and effective relief can be experienced by

Ume is useful to treat many diseases:

A hangover gave this man a monumental headache; he asks himself: "Why did I ever drink so much . . . give me an ume!"

taking an umeboshi in one of the following ways: eat a grilled umeboshi and sip some warm bancha tea; drink some warm water in which an umeboshi has been soaking for five minutes; crush one umeboshi into a small cup of warm water; drink some bancha tea with an umeboshi.

The effective eradication of pain caused by excess drinking has been medically proven. The mechanism is explained as follows: excessive drinking produces too much acidity and causes poor metabolism of minerals. The umeboshi, which is an alkaline food, corrects the acidity imbalance, while the sodium and potassium that it contains activate the metabolism, and as a direct result restores energy and drive to the organism.

9 — ASTHMA

When asthmatic problems occur, take warm lotus root tea with one or two small crushed umeboshi two to three times per day.

10 — MOTION SICKNESS IN CAR, TRAIN, OR AIR

Sucking on an umeboshi will bring quick relief when experiencing any of the above. If taken in advance of the trip, the ume will prevent their occurrence.

11— FLU OR COMMON COLD

It is not possible to catch a cold if an umeboshi is taken daily. If the cold or the flu has already set in, take a well-roasted umeboshi in very hot bancha tea or water as early as possible; it will stop the cold symptoms very effectively.

*Cold and flu symptoms
have you shivering?
Take an ume.*

12 — BURNS

There are three degrees of burns.

    a — First degree burns are superficial and are characterized by an aching redness of the skin.

    b — Second degree burn are deeper and the skin becomes very red and blisters form rapidly.

    c — Third degree burns penetrate and destroy all layers of the skin.

Common household burns are most often of the second degree. For burns of the second degree on any part of the body immediately apply salt water or umeboshi paste. This will effectively prevent the formation of painful blisters. Afterward a light gauze covering soaked with sesame or sunflower oil is placed on the area to promote healing and to prevent permanent scarring.

13 — PTOMAINE OR FOOD POISONING

Ptomaine is most often the result of consuming spoiled animal proteins: eggs, meat, and fish. Poisoning from eating spoiled cereals and vegetables is rare, since pathological organisms and microbes prefer to live in animal protein. Putrefied animal products are much more toxic than decayed vegetables and cereals. Eating spoiled meat or fish can cause severe abdominal pains, vomiting, diarrhea, and fever. The toxic substances formed during the spoilage of animal products are called ptomaine. Summer and fall are the seasons during which more food poisoning occurs. To assure the proper digestion of animal protein, or at the very first sign of intoxication or to assure the proper digestion of animal protein, it is recommended to eat one or more umeboshi or some umeshoban.

PREPARING UMESHOBAN

Cook three crushed umeboshi and three teaspoons of grated ginger in 3 cups of water. Simmer very slowly for twenty minutes. First drink one third of this liquid in order to cause vomiting. Right after that, drink the second cup, this will re-establish the function of the digestive tract that has just been cleared by voiding it. Part of the second cup will also serve to re-establish the function of the central nervous system and the heart. Wait at least one half hour to consume the third umeshoban. This will completely restore the immune mechanism of the organs.

14 — HEADACHES

In former times in Japan, the flesh of an umeboshi plum was applied on the forehead or on the temples whenever someone suffered from a headache. According to ancient Oriental medicine, the temples are the acupuncture points used to heal headaches and facial neuralgia. The ume's active ingredients stimulate this point and increase blood circulation, producing exactly the same beneficial effect.

梅干頭痛膏に梅干番茶は。おばあちゃんの特効薬。

The aging lady wears a small ume plaster adhesive patch on her temple and drinks bancha tea. This is good for female disorders, young or old.

15 — FEVER

Many illnesses are accompanied by fever: Such as colds, bronchitis, tuberculosis, illnesses of digestive organs and contagious diseases. Umeboshi absorbs fever and thus lessens its pain. The very best way to lower the fever is to cause sweating. For this, place one or two partially air dried cabbage leaves on the forehead after drinking one cup of umeshoban. After half an hour the cabbage leaves have absorbed some of the watery perspiration and much of the toxins. Repeat several times and you will feel much better as the fever will drop.

16 — HEMORRHOIDS

For itching, swelling or crevices around the anus, apply that particular part of the body, a cotton cloth that has been soaked in the juice of umeboshi. Since generally the feces of those who eat animal products are quite hard, it must be emphasized that one should suppress these and eat vegetables that contain much cellulose, for instance, root vegetables, in order to facilitate the voiding of the colon.

A sitz bath and a ginger compress are also very effective with hemorrhoids; the ginger, of course, at a low concentration, as follows: Grate about 20 grams of fresh ginger. Put it in a very small cotton sack. Dip this sack in one liter of water, very warm, and allow it to infuse or to soak for a few minutes. Do not boil. dip a rather large piece of cotton in this water. Wring and place on the anus. As soon as it is cold throw it away and begin with a fresh piece of cotton. Change many times during the next twenty minutes. If you add an umeboshi in the warm water the effect will be even greater.

In the case of prolapsus of the rectum one must first take a sitz bath or apply ginger compresses. Then, afterwards, push in and force back in the part that has been dropped after having spread sesame oil on it. It is also very good to take a warm cup of water where the powder of a well roasted umeboshi has been sprinkled. This umeboshi should be the oldest possible. Five year old umeboshi is usually prescribed.

In the case of fistula of the anus it is preferable to apply on the diseased part a product based on a umeboshi. Roast or toast three umeboshi and five winter cherry (coquerets) fruits.[2] Reduce both plums and coquerets into a powder and knead them with a very small amount of sesame oil.

---

2. Coqueret is a perennial plant that has edible red berries; no latin name was given by Dr. Ushio.

17 — VAGINITIS

Caused by the parasite trichomonas vaginalis. Vaginitis is accompanied by loss of white suppuration, hyperemia, and a swelling of the internal mucosa of the vagina. Ordinarily, as in problems in the mouth, the auto-cleansing of the Ume functions well in the vagina. In a healthy individual, the inside of the vagina is normally acid and are host to benefical bacillus that effectively avoid the development of infectious germs.

The decrease in the auto-cleansing capabilities of the body is often caused by the reduction of the ovarian secretion that is strongly influenced by the choice of the daily food. Traditionally, a sitz bath with turnip leaves is very effective in case of vaginitis. But an even more effective way is by adding one or two umeboshi in the warm water of the sitz bath. It is also recommended to introduce in the vagina a cotton pad that has been soaked in the juice of an umeboshi that has been diluted with 7 parts of water.

18 — THE CONTRACEPTIVE METHOD

From the experience of a woman from Osaka, it is reported that a pad of cotton soaked in a water solution of umeboshi extract has been effective as a contraceptive. First a water solution is made from the extract of umeboshi or with crushed fresh umeboshi. One soaks in this solution a cotton pad that has been tied with a very small string. It is placed in the vagina before intercourse.[3]

19 — VOMITING DURING PREGNANCY

Most pregnant women need or wish to take in an acid food such as orange, lemon, or other citrus fruits but usually shun sweet or fat foods. It is a natural tendency for the pregnant woman and, because her fluids invariably tend to acidity, unwittingly she attempts to return to an alkaline condition by eating an acid food.

3. A broad-based, more valid testing of this has not been made in Osaka or anywhere else in Japan, and the continued high birthrate among ume users particularly and macrobiotics generally has not yet confirmed the effectiveness of the ume contraceptive.

Expectant mothers use ume daily during their pregnancy.

In pregnancy the acidity increases even more due to dizzy spells or as discomforts multiply. Not only vomiting and other nauseous sensations occur in the stomach, but the liver function is also decreased. This leaves the future mother completely without any energy. These sicknesses only heighten her moodiness and depression in a very striking manner. Some become hysterical, others become very passive.

This acid condition may even cause the teeth of a pregnant woman to become loose. When the body becomes acid there is a lack of ionized calcium as the future mother is drained of it for the benefit of the fetus. It is at the expense of her teeth that the embryo takes the calcium it needs. However, if she cares for her liver, with an umeboshi a day, the calcium drain will be effectively checked. The consumption of vinegar and other acetic acid foods should be avoided as this leaches calcium from the body but it also makes it more acidic.

20 — VERTIGO DUE TO WEAKNESS OR ANEMIA

Young people, especially young working women suffer from severe anemia manifested by dizziness and sometimes even loss of consciousness. The cause may be a lowering of the red blood cells or the result of illnesses that are accompanied by hemorrhaging: stomach ulcers, intestinal, anal or uterine disorders. Widespread consumption of refined flour products, sweets, tropical fruits and spicy foods are the major causes of anemia. A swift and efficient remedy is the taking of umeshoban, a change to the macrobiotic way of eating, and rest.

21- RADIATION EXPOSURE AND X-RAY OVERDOSE

The atomic bomb killed 100,000 people in Hiroshima at the end of World War II. However the entire staff and all of the patients of a Catholic hospital within the bomb's effective radius were miraculously saved, while nearly all other residents of that area perished. The survivors owed their lives to the practice of macrobiotics under the able direction of Dr. T. Akizuki who treated his charges daily with umeboshi as a preventive measure. Another medical doctor, Dr. Hazakawa states that the umeboshi was needed to prevent the spread of illnesses that occured in the aftermath of atomic fallout from the lingering radioactivity. In his book, Dr. M. K. Mihashi wrote that the umeboshi effectively cured a woman whose white blood cells were diminishing drastically to the point that death was imminent. Fully recovered within six months her health was excellent.

Strontium 90, within the past 40 to 50 years, has been the cause of many problems. So much strontium 90 accumulated in the rice fields of Japan that it became cause for concern. As it concentrates mainly in the outer bran coats, the amount was actually higher in whole brown rice than in polished white rice, this caused many macrobiotic persons in Japan to shun brown rice. This however was an over reaction, because as Dr I. Numata discovered, the phytic acid in the bran facilitates the elimination of strontium 90 from the body of the consumer. Further Dr. Numata determined that the problem is resolved to complete satisfaction by adding an ume while cooking the brown rice.

22 - ECZEMA, ATHLETE'S FOOT
OR SWEATY FEET

Before the western style footwear became popular in Japan, the problem of athlete's foot never existed, because zoris and getas (wooden shoes) were worn exclusively before that. However, as many Japanese began to adopt occidental clothing and food habits, eating meat as well as wearing oxfords and other closed toes shoes, athletes foot became widespread. Even today, no specific medication exists for these particular ailments but I have personally known people who suffered for over ten years from these ailments. With the practice of macrobiotics, they were able to cure the condition. From the macrobiotic point of view, eczema and athlete's foot develop or become aggravated when the condition becomes yin. When the basic standard macrobiotic diet is widened or forgotten, these liberties cause an immediate recurrence of the problem. This is essentially a blood cleansing problem. As a symptomatic remedy, spread ume plum paste on the affected part, allow it to penetrate in the skin, then apply a light coating of sesame oil mixed with a small amount of ginger juice. Additionally, those who suffer from any kind of skin problem should never wear any synthetic socks or underwear.

23 - INFANT'S TROUBLE AT NIGHT

There are many reasons to make a baby cry during the night. Possible causes are that the diaper may be wet or soiled, or that too much food or milk was given shortly before retiring. An erratic time table will create poor eating habits; this in turn might cause a slower general development of the nervous system and the brain. Without allowing the practice to become a daily necessity, an ume enema should be given as follows: 20 cc. of water containing 1/2 gram of umeboshi extract.

Pickling the Ume

Let us now examine how the umeboshi salted plum
is made in the cottage industry of Japan.

The late doctor of letters, Dr. K. Mizumi, Ph.D., was known to be a
master in making umeboshi, even though it was only a hobby for
him. He often said: "Among the various methods of preservation
the best is the pickling of umeboshi." "In our country and in our
own family," said Dr. Mizumi, "we have never eaten an umeboshi
that was less than ten years old.

According to my mother the umeboshi should have at least one
hundred years of age in order to have a good quality. At this
particular time the flesh becomes so transparent that the pit can be
seen through the plum flesh. In 1927 I ate an umeboshi that came
from the very same vat from which my grandfather helped himself
to take along a few umeboshis as protection during the Battle of
Tobakufushi in 1868." I would like to outline for you now the
Mizumi method for making umeboshi.

First, the right timing of when to pick the fruit. Some have said
that the ideal moment was the third day after the beginning of the
rainy season, which is the 11th of June. However, Mr. Mizumi
would rather begin on the tenth day after the beginning of the rainy
season. The more juice the plums can produce during the pickling
process the better they will taste.

The plums should be culled and sorted and then soaked in water containing rice bran for two nights and two days. The plums then become yellow. On the third day they are washed well, then drained. Following that, one begins to preserve them with salt. Normally, one utilizes a proportion of 0.36 liter of pure natural salt for 1.8 liters of plums. In the Orient, traditionally, the salt, plum, water, etc. are measured according to volume rather than by weight.

Famous in Japan for his military leadership, Hideyoshi Toyotomi would shout to his tired foot soldiers: "Right over that mountain, there is a Japanese Plum tree grove!" This galvanized his troops and made them hasten the pace. Because of his use of Ume plums in the lowly foot soldier's daily rations and his military strategy, this general ranked in popularity with the Emperor.

ONLY NATURAL SALT
SHOULD BE USED FOR PICKLING

Today it is difficult to obtain natural salt in Japan. Refined salt is often used in daily life, but this has been refined by such a physico-chemical process that it is far from being natural.

Vegetables or plums pickled in this or any refined salt will not keep well since this salt lacks many essential elements including nigari (bitters). Nigari is the bitter part of natural gray seasalt which contains magnesium, calcium and potassium. These elements are anti-putrefactive and essential to insure the good keeping quality of the pickled plums.

The amniotic fluid which nourishes the embryo contains essential minerals in the same proportion as sea water. Shellfish cannot live in water salted only with 100% refined soldium chloride in solution. When pickling umeboshi, it is very important that the pickling brine be made with natural salt since it contains the bitters (rich in magnesium salts). One should use an average of 150 grams of Celtic natural salt or 200 grams of refined white salt for 1 kilo of plums.

The most ideal container is a shallow wooden barrel. After having copiously sprinkled the prunes with salt, they are placed in this low sided-vat. One then lays a round wooden plank on top in direct contact with the plums and a heavy rock is placed on top of that. Of course, there is a relationship between the weight of the rock and the plums. The weight of the stone must be equal to or more than the weight of the plums themselves. If the stone is too light the juice will not come out and the plums will harden.

Two or three days of stone pressure on top and the juice will rise up above the plank and the stone. One skims off and discards this juice. The plums are then aged until the 21st of July. During the intervening time, you must proceed to the preparation of the shiso leaves, *perilla frutescens* in Latin.

Normally one uses only the red shiso, or akaziso, to color the plums. However, Dr. Mizumi recommends mixing the red shiso with the curly or chirimen shiso, because in this particular case the color becomes much more vivid. Following that, one tears the leaves of the shiso plant into small pieces, puts them in a large bowl, and sprinkles them with a small amount of salt and bruise them lightly. At that time a dark green juice which contains all of the bitterness of the plant comes out of the leaves. This bitter juice must be discarded.

THE SECRET OF MAKING QUALITY UMEBOSHI

The quality of the umeboshi depends on more than just the right choice of the raw ingredients: from the choice of the plum's varietal quality, the naturalness of the salt and the proper species of shiso.

One must also take into consideration three most important criteria that affect the quality of the umeboshi plum itself:

1) size and species of plum;
2) region of production;
3) degree of ripeness of the plum.

The size of the plum varies according to the species. For the manufacture of umeboshi it is best to choose a medium or small plum. The species Shiro-kaga is appreciated by everyone, because its flesh is soft and its skin is not too thick.

The thinness of skin or inside softness of the plum depends upon the climate and geographical area of production. The skin of the southern region plum is thin and its flesh is very soft, whereas in the north the reverse is true. Umeboshi picklers generally prefer plums from the warmer parts of the country.

Ripe plums cannot be used to make pickled umeboshi. The skin of ripe plums too often tears when the pickling is begun, yielding an ume of bad quality. These ripe plums can be used only for making plum jam. Many years of experience are necessary in order to judge the degree of ripeness, and it is difficult to exactly gauge when the ideal maturity has been reached.

THE SYMBIOSIS BETWEEN UME AND THE SHISO PLANT

Shiso: Shiso is a plant (*perilla frutescens*) also called Perrilla of Nanking, a city in China. School children often ask this question of their teachers. "Why and how does the green plum become a red umeboshi?" This is one of Nature's interesting transformations. Even umeboshi experts continue to become excited at the sight of this change of color when the juice of shiso leaves and the juice of salted plums first blend.

The man with the lance is surrounded by menacing ugly bacteria and germs. His shield plate says "Shiso". Shiso leaves not only color the ume plums but also serve to ward off harmful organisms.

Shiso contains anthocyan, a substance which, when combined with malic, citric, or tartaric acid of the plums, gives the finished umeboshi plums their characteristic red coloring and their therapeutic quality. The longer the plums stay together with shiso, the redder they will turn.

The shiso plant is an annual. The shiso leaf contains much of vitamins A, C, and B_2, and is also rich in calcium, iron, phosphorus, and other minerals. One finds this plant everywhere in Japan and, although it is of Chinese origin, it grows wild in some parts of California. For the past three centuries it has been utilized for the pickling of umeboshi. Many species of shiso exist, such as Akaziso (red shiso), Aziso (green shiso), Chirimen (curly red shiso), Ao-chirimen (curly green shiso), etc. The red shiso must be used in order to color the umeboshi in the familiar shade.

Shiso generally reaches a height of 30 to 80 centimeters, or between 15 and 30 inches. Its white flowers bloom between summer and fall. It has strong vitality, requires no care, and grows freely, just like wild herbs. However, it is very bitter. This gives it great sterilizing power, estimated by experts to be one thousand times stronger than formaldehyde.

In June or July wash and drain the leaves, then measure the shiso volume and add 10% of coarse seasalt that is rubbed into the shiso leaves. Throw away the juice that is released, since it contains all the shiso bitterness. If this juice is utilized by mistake, the umeboshi will turn black rather than red.

Three of Japan's prefectures chose the Ume blossom as their state flower, one of these prefectures is Fukuoka in Kyushu. One thousand years ago, Mishizane Sugawara was an exiled warrior who wrote a poem about the fragrance of the Ume flower. He is also famous as a symbol of learning; today, college students pay homage to him in the hopes of getting better grade at exam time. A Kuyshu shrine honors him.

Normally the volume of shiso leaves used represents between 5% and 10% of the weight of the plums. Shiso leaves dried until the end of July become more and more red due to the action of the sun's ultraviolet rays. Besides its anti-putrefactive character, shiso also contains much linoleic acid, which positively dissolves the excess cholesterol that causes arteriosclerosis.

The flavor of this plant stimulates appetite; this is why, for a long time now, I have always mixed shiso leaves finely cut into match sticks size into salads, or I incorporate them in miso soup. Both recipes seem to help revive lagging appetites.

Oriental medicine teaches us that the shiso plant has many medicinal benefits. It calms and tranquilizes the nervous system, stimulates healthful perspiration, possesses diuretic properties, facilitates the work of the digestive system, and cures food poisoning caused by the eating of crab, other shellfish, and meat. It is also very effective in stopping a cold or coughing.

The juice of raw shiso leaves is also effective in fighting ringworm infection and herpes, which are very contagious skin diseases, the first being caused by the Trichophyton rubrum or even Trichophyton schoenleini. This fungus infects superficial tissues such as the skin, hair, and nails of man and animals. It primarily affects the scalp of children with lots of hair, but can also affect adolescents until age 20.

THE PRACTICAL MAKING OF THE UMEBOSHI

On the 21st of July the plums are ready to be dried in the sun. First wring the shiso leaves directly above the vat so that not one drop of the precious juice is lost. Dry the leaves on a plank outside. Take a large bamboo basket and place it over an oversized bowl to collect all drippings.

Every one of these plums goes into this basket above so that all the juice will be caught below. After letting them drain well, place them one by one and not touching each other on a plank outside in the sun and let them dry. At this particular stage it is important to watch the weather because the plums cannot be exposed to rain.

Let them dry the first day, even overnight, to make them even more tender. This exposes them to both the morning and evening dew. Very early the next morning roll the plums, now moistened with dew, on boards in order to moisten them well with the dew in homogenous fashion, then continue to dry them for that day.

From the very first day you've exposed the juice found at the bottom of the bowl to the sun. Once the plums are dried put them in this moist warm juice so they can absorb a sufficient amount, and put the shiso leaves on top of the plums.

Remove the plums from the vat again the next day to let them dry on the bamboo basket; repeat the whole process of the previous days. It is said traditionally that the plums should dry for three days and three nights during the heat of summer.

However, according to Mr. Mizumi, this is not sufficient. These operations should be repeated seven days in a row at the height of summer's heat.

Today in Japan, the sight of tree blossoms conjures up the image of cherry blossoms. But over a thousand years ago, it meant Ume blossoms. The short poem at left of the figure: "I live in a high mountain village where Ume trees blossom while snow begins to fall."

HOW TO TELL A GOOD QUALITY UME

The signs of a quality are the luster of the plum and the transparency of its meat.

The skin of the plum should have a rather dark coloring and a very good springiness. This signifies that these plums have an abundant flesh inside. Umeboshi are better when they have more flesh or when the seeds are smaller.

Until recently in Japan, the very best umeboshis were those made in the province of Wakayama. Criterion of taste is defined by the proportion between the salt and the acidity . An umeboshi that does not taste salty but rather tastes sweet is not a good one. The acid taste must dominate, and the very best umeboshi is acid and possesses a clean fresh taste at the very same time.

Epilogue:

From China to Japan to California

The pickled fruits of *Prunus Mumé,* or Umeboshi were in widespread use in China a long time ago. Japanese travelers and monks exploring the vast chinese empire brought back the usage and some seedlings of the medicinal wonder tree back to their homeland. Soon the fruits of the Mumé became a household word in their new country. Thirteen centuries ago the Mumé (or Ume) tree was so well acclimatized to Japan that it began to grow wild. To guard against any import by other countries, the translation of Umeboshi as "salt plums" was a clever Japanese invention that kept secret the origin of one of Japan's most prized rediscovered treasure of gastronomy and folk medicine.

The Ume is a most versatile and useful condiment for steamed or boiled vegetables. It is also the main condiment and natural preservative in the popular lunch boxes of the Orient, and it is now slowly gaining acceptance in the Western world. Its delicious sour taste adds an interesting and habit-forming taste to various dishes, making them easier to digest and more refreshing. Even in the warmest season, it prevents spoilage and keeps rice fresh and tasty.

Over 100 years ago, the Japanese Ume became a cultivated commercial crop on the sunny plains and hilltops of the Wakayama

region. The demands for export of the Ume began a commercializa-
tion that required new technologies, harvesting methods and even
the introduction of chemical additives. All of these innovations
resulted in a very marked alteration in the quality of Umeboshi
when compared to the home-grown and home pickled product. The
hand sorting of the fruit is now frequently done by machines in the
large enterprises. The deep wooden kegs have been replaced by
concrete tanks lined with fiberglass, six tons of fruits are thus
processed at a time and highly refined salt is routinely used. Since
salt represents about 20 to 30 % of the weight of the prepared fruit,
the commercial product is greatly diminished in its benefits and the
therapeutic effects of the Ume. It is true that the refined salt is
"mellowed" by time, the tartness of the shiso leaves and the citric
acid, but the lack of the macro- and trace minerals in hydrolysis-
refining of salt is a factor to be seriously considered when choosing
Umeboshi.

Ume Trees Bloom in California

For some twenty years now a resolute Japanese man dedicated to
natural agriculture has had a dream: To grow and prepare (preserve)
umeboshis in the U.S. The hardships he and his wife endured to
finally realize that dream would make good reading and actually
parallel the story of "The Man who Planted Hope and Grew Happi-
ness."[1]

   After several unsuccessful attempts in Chico, California and in
Bellevue, Washington, Junsei Yamazaki and his wife Kazuko fi-
nally settled in Orland, California where the small model farm they
run in that fertile valley is a lesson in commitment and a jewel to
behold.

   The pioneer spirit that animates the Yamazakis has created a
few firsts. It is at their farm that tender rice seedlings are planted by
hand into the flooded paddies. This has demonstrated the superior
food energy that rice planted by hand could offer to many here in
the U.S. Every Spring, friends from many parts of the world gather
at the farm and cheerfully work ankle-deep in the mud of the paddy

1. See the book by that title, published by Happiness Press.

field. The same crew, swollen by a few more volunteers, returns in the Fall to harvest an outstanding crop of the tastiest and most nourishing cereal grain.

Harvesting hand planted rice at Junsei's farm is a task that fills us with gratitude and peace.

The vegetable patch yields an abundant selection of oriental, european and american classics with the strength and flavor usually found only in wild vegetables.

A subtle demonstration, unspoken but very present, tells about the effect of this kinship with the soil. It quietly shows that a reverence for nature invariably breeds the finest human spirit: The calm couple who tend this farm extend the warmest welcome to all comers with the sort of genuine openness that is in sharp contrast with the proverbial inscrutable mind.

For the past three years a handsome orchard of ume trees has proliferated at the entrance to the farm. In early Spring, visitors are greeted by a white and pink blossoms explosion.

The cover of the present book displays not only the blossoms but one of the many hard working bees as well. Pollination was going on as usual this Spring but little coaxing was needed to obtain a photograph of the bee as it drank the mellow nectar. For anyone who has ever tasted Junsei's Ume plums, the sweetness is built-in, a result of the considerate attitude described above.

Junsei and Kazuko Yamazaki as they appear in cartoon on the Ume and Miso labels.

Close attention to the quality of ingredients is another Yamazaki secret that bears scrutiny: In his method for making umes, Dr. Ushio tells us that nothing but the best natural salt will pickle the Ume correctly. Junsei and Kazuko insist on using only the light gray Celtic seasalt of French origin for preserving their Ume pickle as well as for their natural miso fermentation. This is easily detected in both products by their superior taste and the rapid renewal of energy experienced when consuming the miso and the plums. It far surpasses any other imported miso or Ume. As all home-grown products, the supply is limited and in this particular instance, the quality has created a highly loyal following. Purposely, we have refrained from giving the address or phone for these hard working biological farmers. We kindly ask that you respect their time with consideration for the many chores they must perform to produce the farm products that are so beneficial to health and peace.

Recipes Using Umeboshi

Rice Cooked with Umeboshi

5 cups of brown rice
4 whole umeboshi, torn into small pieces
2 or 3 shiso leaves

Soak the rice one hour in cold water then drain before cooking; then add 6 cups of water and the umeboshi. Cook them with their pits but remove them after cooking. Garnish with the shiso leaves.

Rice Porridge

2 cups of brown rice
20 cups of water
2 or 3 umeboshi
a small palm full of 3 year twig tea

Roast the tea and put it in a cotton bag. Bring the water and tea to a boil, then remove the cotton bag. Pour the rice into the warm water and cook it with the umeboshi.

This is a traditional and much appreciated recipe that comes from the region where umeboshi are grown.

Potage of Umeboshi
(serves one person)

1 gram of grated bonito

1 teaspoon of tamari

1 umeboshi

1/2 sheet of nori, cut into small pieces

Place the umeboshi, tamari, and bonito into a large cup or bowl. Add boiling water and the nori. This preparation is instantaneous and banishes fatigue very rapidly.

Umeboshi Sandwich

12 slices of naturally leavened bread

3 umeboshi

3 radishes, cut into small pieces

6 finely shredded green salad leaves

Remove the pits from the umeboshi and grind the fleshy part into a paste. Mix it with the radishes and the salad leaves. Spread this mixture on the 2 slices of bread.

Umeboshi Fritters
Beignets d'Umeboshi — (serves 6)

6 umeboshis

1 beaten egg

2 tbsp. freshly ground whole wheat flour or whole wheat bread crumbs

Soak the umeboshi in warm water for one hour; let drain and sprinkle with flour. Dip them in the beaten egg, roll in flour or bread crumbs, and fry.

Nituke of Fish

6 mackerel, sardines, or tuna pieces

3 umeboshi

3 teaspoons tamari

Clean the fish, remove the waste and cook the filet with the umeboshi, simmer on low to medium heat Season with tamari.

Calamari with Umeboshi

300 grams of calamari

1 cucumber

3 umeboshi

1 teaspoon tamari

Soak the umeboshi overnight. Take out the fine membrane of the calamari and cut them into little squares of under an inch. Let them simmer in 1 teaspoon of white wine on low flame.

Cut the cucumbers lengthwise into four pieces, then in pieces 1/2 inch long. Remove the umeboshi pits and mash the flesh with tamari and a small amount of white wine or mirin. Mix the cucumbers, calamary, tamari, and umeboshi and serve.

Wakame with Umeboshi

3 umeboshi

3 grams grated bonito

60 grams wakame sea vegetable

Remove the umeboshi pits and mash their flesh with the grated bonito. Dip the wakame into warm water for a few minutes and them cut it. Mix with the ume mixture.

Instant Vegetable Preserves

1/2 cabbage, finely chopped

3 to 4 umeboshi, pits removed and flesh mashed

1 small carrot, cut into fine match sticks

20 grams of kombu sea vegetables, washed and cut into slender pieces 1 1/2 in. long.

Soak kombu in warm water for 5 minutes. Mix all these ingredients in a salad bowl. Let sit 3 hours while under pressure: a wooden board can be placed on top of the vegetables, and a large stone on top of that. A salad press may be used also.

The above may be used immediately (within 3 hours) but is even more delicious when aged for one or more days.

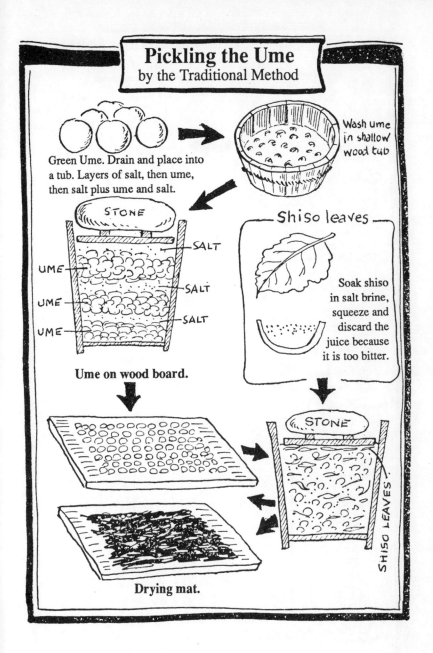

Pickling the Ume
by the Traditional Method

Green Ume. Drain and place into a tub. Layers of salt, then ume, then salt plus ume and salt.

Wash ume in shallow wood tub

STONE

SALT

UME
UME
UME

SALT
SALT

Ume on wood board.

Shiso leaves

Soak shiso in salt brine, squeeze and discard the juice because it is too bitter.

STONE

SHISO LEAVES

Drying mat.

Making Ume Plum Wine
by the Traditional Method

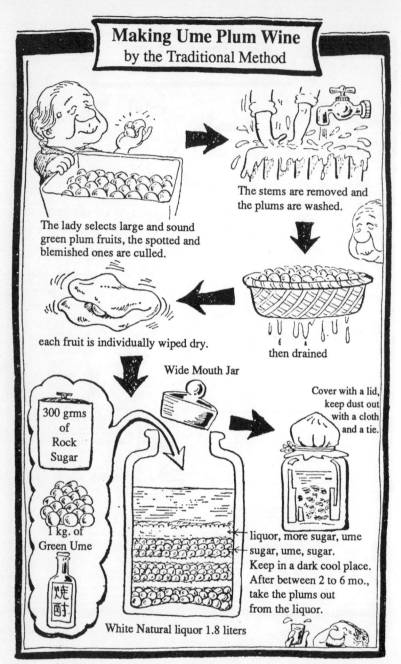

The lady selects large and sound green plum fruits, the spotted and blemished ones are culled.

The stems are removed and the plums are washed.

each fruit is individually wiped dry.

then drained

Wide Mouth Jar

300 grms of Rock Sugar

1 kg. of Green Ume

White Natural liquor 1.8 liters

焼酎

Cover with a lid, keep dust out with a cloth and a tie.

liquor, more sugar, ume sugar, ume, sugar. Keep in a dark cool place. After between 2 to 6 mo., take the plums out from the liquor.

Use (raw) rock sugar as white refined dissolves too quickly and does not draw out plum flavor.

38